Fossil Record
Wayne Price

smith|doorstop

Published 2015 by
smith|doorstop Books
The Poetry Business
Bank Street Arts
32-40 Bank Street
Sheffield S1 2DS

Copyright © Wayne Price 2015
All Rights Reserved

ISBN 978-1-910367-46-9
Typeset by Utter
Printed by MPG Biddles

Acknowledgements
Acknowledgements are due to the following publications where some of these poems, or versions of them, have appeared: *Acumen, CAST: The Poetry Business Book of New Contemporary Poets* (smith|doorstop), *Causeway/Cabhsair, Orbis, Stone* (Wyvern Works), *The Fish Anthology 2013* (Fish Publishing), *New Writing Scotland 29 & 30* (ASLS), *Northwords Now, The North*. 'Vacanti's Mouse' was runner-up in the inaugural Edwin Morgan International Poetry Competition 2008; 'Surfers, Carrowmore Strand' won the Torbay Open Poetry Competition 2011; 'Crows, Seaton Park' won the Poetry on the Lake International Poetry Competition 2012; 'Nightfishing', 'Witness' and 'Suburban Gardens at Night' were finalists in the 2013 Manchester Poetry Prize; 'Prayer', 'The Guests' and 'In European Woods' were finalists in the 2014 Manchester Poetry Prize.

smith|doorstop Books are a member of Inpress:
www.inpressbooks.co.uk. Distributed by Central Books Ltd.,
99 Wallis Road, London E9 5LN

The Poetry Business gratefully acknowledges the support
of Arts Council England.

Contents

5	Nightfishing
6	Loyalties
7	Helpless
9	In European Woods
10	Witness
11	Vacanti's Mouse
12	Prayer
13	Crows, Seaton Park
15	Heads of the Valleys
18	Hey Water
19	Allotment
20	High Bridge
21	Surfers, Carrowmore Strand
22	Suburban Gardens at Night
23	Fossil Record
24	Grasshoppers, June
25	The Weather at the End of the News
27	The Guests
28	Dead Hawk, the Anglican Churchyard, Tangier
30	Not the Place but How the Place Was Found

For my mother and father

Nightfishing

Hand and mind are fishing the river after dark
for the slow, heavy old ones that rise at night.

The white feathers on the hook are spread
like wings on a moth. Mind watches them travel down

the bright lane the moon makes. A white moon and the white bait.
The line in hand grows heavy with the river's black weight.

Or it is an indoor scene: the moon's fluorescent silver on the stream
is the night light over beds in the emergency room.

In the deepest pools the trout, heavy as sacks of sand,
are swaying in their gravel bowls, between the big stones.

Their bodies shape their homes. They have fattened
on smaller shapes that were images of their own.

Hand and mind are fishing for a nest of forms.
Like an egg in a nest of clouds, the moon.

The bait is a moth that has battened on the window pane.
As mind stares out, it stares in. Like chains the hooks and lines

of drugs and salt and blood to hands. Mind is fishing between
the banks of beds. Like moonlight, one light always on.

Loyalties

Sometimes I think it's the uncanniness of animals
draws us to them; the blacked out,
unfurnished rooms of their eyes, a liquid
indifference to the suffering
of others of their kind. And the miraculous
weightlessness of cattle and horses;
so much heavier-boned than us
and no weary heaviness at all of self.

I remember, though, our one and only dog,
a recovered stray, rescued from a schoolyard
where he'd paddled for days, nose-up,
in tides of kids, and who dislocated
both hind legs by hurling himself
at our kitchen door all night.
He'd wanted to sleep
in sight of us, on the bedroom floor.

We couldn't let him, we'd agreed: it would be
a slippery slope he'd soon slide down
to land in bed between us, and how would we
break the habit then?
We thought the howling was just frustration
until we found him at seven, writhing,
his mouth spilling foam. In his agony
he'd gnashed up half the lino.

He didn't have to come between us in the end.
When I left to rent a single room
I couldn't take him. And you
were out at work all day:
he'd have chewed the house down.
Twenty five years. Ah, God.
Wouldn't we let him sleep in peace
anywhere he wanted now?

Helpless

August afternoon. I'd flung
the back door of my grandparents'
narrow, lean-to kitchen open, expecting sunshine
in their sunken concrete yard.
                          The stale air seethed
into life and sound, the machine snarl
of bluebottles, swirling and batting
at my face and hands
as if tumbled
in a nightmarish snow globe.
The twelve white ducks
my grandfather had reared
for months on mash and meal
were dead. Each bird,
hanging like terrible
laundry by its legs, smiled raggedly
at the neck, where the blood had been let.
I stared at the jellied puddle
where each of their lives had mixed
and levelled. It was glossy as the top
of an old-fashioned casket, shellacked
to a rosy black.

Now that I was still, the flies
settled again:
furring the flat wet disk of blood,
clasping like brooches
on the opened throats.
I remembered the fat mild ducks
in life, following me up and down the path, gabbling
sociably in the mud.

When I moved at all
the host of flies like rioters
boiled up again. For a while
I made a game of it,
conducting them like God.
Beyond the yard, in the allotment above,
I could hear my grandfather whistling
his pigeons round and round,
circle after circle
in the blue sky overhead. In front of me
the broken outhouse stared, shaggy and dark
in its pelt of ivy, its rotten door
gaping open
on one bad hinge.

And suddenly I felt
the strange helplessness in all of it:
the useless door like a twisted mouth
that hadn't shut for years
and now never would; the flies
that could not stop themselves
obeying my commands; the pigeons wheeling
on invisible tracks, their awful, obedient
repetitions; my kindly, weak-eyed
grandmother, even, somewhere
in a dim, crooked room indoors,
knitting, knitting, knitting
things we'd never want to wear;
and the ducks with their friendly, blunt-beaked
heads, that used to follow where I led, dangling
now above a pond of blood, absurdly
upside-down in air, helplessly dead.

In European Woods

Slowly the morning light
gives back the bedroom walls,
releases the world
object by object, giving up
the colours last of all.

Mornings like these
there are European woods
where the folk tales still
begin, begin again
their country meanings, in monochrome.

One by one, amongst
wolf-pack and bear, deserters
from three thousand years
of armies have bivouacked there,
where ceilings are branches

of pine and juniper. Under
their shelter, in what is left
of uniforms – Macedonian
bronze, furs from the steppes
of Scythia, the field-grey

of *Panzergruppen* – voices
in a snow-hushed, perpetual dawn
murmur in Latin,
or the Greek of Byzantium,
and other languages long gone.

Witness

I've followed the older boys stealing milk
from doorsteps at dawn, after long pale nights
in summer spent camping on the rugby ground.
When they took them from my own front door
I never complained. And I watched them hang
a screaming friend of mine by his ankles from
the quarry cliff, then watched him hoisted back again.

I've stood and watched as Benny Griffiths took
a kicking that nearly killed him, outside
the Workingmen's Hall. He curled inwards like a snail
until the toes of those big boots had picked
his skinny body loose like string; I watched
by the cenotaph, late, in the rain. Years
I've watched myself watching. These and other things.

Vacanti's Mouse

> *'The mouse, hairless and specially bred to lack an*
> *immune system that might reject the human tissue, nourishes*
> *the ear as the cartilage cells grow.'*

Always bored, like Adam
if God had forgotten Eve and naming,

I imagined my aching spine
under a sail of gristle and skin; voices in

horse latitudes of sterile laboratory air
teased it like the promise of freedom or

change. Nothing ever changed
of course, except the steady, strange

unfurling of its growth; wing-bud;
soft sea-shell; whatever image wobbled

in the dim steel mirror of my
water-bowl. It grew like any metaphor: sly

parasite, cancer, transfiguration;
and though the burden of human hearing

has been hard on me, a heavy dream,
I think that doomed horses, massy and dumb,

flung helpless into perfect blue for men,
knew something of my own exhilaration

when the miracle, the shivering edge
of my nakedness, first filled with your language.

Prayer

The past is always watching; curtains
twitching in the windows of its model houses
that are small enough to lodge
in a toddler's nostril. On their miniature
rooftops a remembered sun
is always glinting after remembered rain.

I have become
like one of those sad, grown men
who must keep his children away
from the delicate train-set in the attic;
the mouse-sized, pristine engines in Edwardian
reds and greens; toothpick trees as brittle as icing.

What kind of game, exactly,
is this, that only makes us understand
just how clumsy we've become – all thumbs – breaking
everything we touch, in time? I see
Clive Terrace, its bending road as thin
as a coat-hanger's wire neck. And with a sound

as faint as the tick of a watch
one of the tiny doors is opening. Why
did we never look up and see
our own-shaped shadows across the mountain?
Could we ever hear, anyway, from this terrible
height, what our own small voices are shouting?

Crows, Seaton Park

The green of afternoon
is spooling backwards to grey. Flats
of water on the football pitch
mirror like tin.

I have counted
twenty-nine crows on the playing field,
upright, silent, discretely spaced,
professionally still.
They have clasped
their wings behind their backs
like undertakers' hands.

What are they waiting for?
They ignore the faint sounds
of the last of the children
dropping to their feet
from the climbing frames; the voices
of mothers pushing prams.

Finally, like a man
remembering the time, one
flaps toward the woods
and disappears.

All around
a heaviness has landed,
like a great, inexplicable craft,
its landing gear
acres wide, sinking
through the evening air
onto flooded ground,
onto slides and benches, onto creaking,

stiff-chained swings;
the crows taking
flight at first, then settling, incurious,
on its cooling wings.

Heads of the Valleys

i

The car is ticking as it cools, seems
lost in thought, the way the rooms
of a house in the small black hours
settle into themselves
in our absence. I have
eased my way along a steep
lane of snow, tip-toed four unsteady tyres
over the slippery clatter of a cattle grid
and shrieked an ice-
bound gate to get here
from the Heads of the Valleys road.

ii

The moon is a thumb-print in chalk
on a window that has all the navy
night behind. Like the riding lights
of ferries and freighters,
the lamps of the valleys' towns
sail out on the hills' fixed waves, the fossiled
winter swell of Rhondda Fach and Rhondda Fawr.

iii

I remember school friends who went early
to work underground, how they
boasted to those of us left behind
in classrooms and rain
of paying for a girl, or Blackpool
weekend, or down-payment on a car,
by opening a two-inch seam
on the back of a hand, and forcing the coal dust
under the skin; easy compensation
for a lifetime scar.

iv

The scurrying river behind the surgery
was always changing its mind:
sometimes black, sometimes brown.
Every evening it fed the Cynon
another rope of liquorice.
Standing on the waiting room's
narrow wooden bench, I watched it
through the window, my milk-toothed breath
fogging the glass, my grandfather's hand
steadying my legs. The waiting room
was always too cold or too hot, and all the men
my grandfather knew spoke the same wet cough.

v

I could almost hear my name
in the creak of the washery's
gantries in the wind. Now, the patient
salmon are back, leaping the weirs each spring
at Radyr and Troedyrhiw
after a hundred years of waiting.
Tonight, the clear moon on their smooth
slow pools must be white and round
and hard to swallow
as an old-fashioned pill, something spilled
from a dark, Victorian jar.

vi

My grandparents sometimes brought us here
Sunday afternoons in summer: their grey,
goggle-eyed Morris Minor
baking in the sun. 1969.
Tinned salmon sandwiches, the tall
red thermos of sweet tea;
the roll of the land
opening like the leaves
of a child's encyclopedia of guesses.

vii

My own car
is dreaming on a page of snow, as if it had
nowhere to go. I scrape
its throat with the key; it blinks awake
like an animal.   I could drive
anywhere now, follow the anchored
lightships to Cardiff
or drift aboard the slim bright
bridge beyond, swaying
on its strings, and find a country
between remedy
and compensation. Beyond
children, beyond a lifetime, what marks
it leaves and doesn't leave;
beyond those
children's children.

Hey Water

Ten years now you've been gone. This morning, a boy
of three or four, loud and brassy as a school bell,
raced round the back of this farmhouse hotel
and saw the bright zinc pipe that bleeds water
from the heavy hill and splashes it to an open drain.

I was back there to smoke a cigarette. I nodded
and said hello but it was only the clatter of falling
water he listened to. He froze and watched it flare in the sun.
Hey water! Where you going? he yelled, then spun away
at once of course, having no interest in the answer.

Allotment

We were turning that too heavy earth too long,
too long and at the wrong time –
days of rain had made a world of clay that clung
to our spades, gripped like misery.

Why were we digging so long and so late?
It was autumn, it was night,
and I can't see my father beside me
even in memory.

Why was it he would not stop
and scrape our spades' steel faces clean
on the heel of his black boot?
What kept us from home?

And what use was I there,
as if with a toothpick
to roll a weight that felt
the whole drowned deadweight of the globe?

The dark was all one clay
that fastened sky and leaves and roots; I knew
that canopies of oak and beech
repeat themselves inside the soil.

Behind the eye the brain's white branches
work so hard to right the world. Boy or man
in the dark, who is still in that allotment
leaning blind into the work?

High Bridge

I out-stared a fox at ten
paces today, on the ghost line
above the Spean where the one-track
railway used to run between
Fort Augustus and Fort William,

at what's left of High Bridge
where a piper and twelve shouting men
stopped eighty soldiers crossing, shot dead
three of them and sent the others running
along the green way I was walking.

A quarter of an ever more murderous
millennium since then, and Wade's
military bridge, both arches
long gone, is a half-done puzzle
of masonry and tangled iron.

I smoked a cigarette, stared down
at the swallowing black river
unravelling after rain. Across it,
on the steep far bank in May sun, a few
silent sheep, a few unsteady lambs

grazing between the birch-wood's
white, short-lived trunks
that were wet still – though the weather
on the corries and the Great Glen
was clearing – unreachable, gleaming.

Surfers, Carrowmore Strand

Lowry might have painted these
simple lives in the foam; approximate
black stick-figures, flocked as if for company
but absorbedly separate and alone.

Their brief paths cross over crumbling ruins.
Most lie flat, can barely evolve
to crouch or kneel, slide open-mouthed, face-on
into a simmer that is nobody's

land, that shifts its million territories
moment by moment under them.
The sea is too big for some; they tire
and stagger ashore, one by one. Others

grow younger, flinging themselves sideways
as they fall, as if blasted out of the water.
They are always choosing the wrong wave,
but simply choose another; are so content

to get so little right. They are disappearing
in a white moment that comes
again and again. They are practicing
abandoning everything, everyone.

Suburban Gardens at Night

are a country of their own,
belonging to no-one. Evening after evening
they repossess themselves, at the moment
the kitchen light snaps on
and blinds us to everything
beyond itself.

Why would we even want to be
out there, alone with them,
in their pale, other-worldly no-man's land
of small dry moons, abandoned slabs?

There is always
a colourless mirror-lawn
of fine tough roots
under the grass. It drinks up darkness
the way green leaves drink light.
Nobody wants
the thought of it, that other, white garden,
so close beneath the one
they think of as their own; those million limp
blind drinkers staring down.

I bend to stub my cigarette
on a paving stone. The cement path is speckled
like a hedge bird's egg
with the first few drops of rain.
Two houses along, a bathroom light
is shining. The sound of running water,
then darkness again.

Fossil Record

Wind was stammering at the windows all night.
If I slept at all it was a half-sleep
filled with thoughts that halved into dreams
and back again. The first cells divided
identically, for millions of years.
Millions of years before difference began.

Slow learning life. Slower than stone. I would
like a sleep as deep as those first fractal
animals, colourless, rooted in the dark
of empty oceans, carbon-paper thin.

Everything in the wind says give me time,
I can change: minerals in the rocks and streams;
proteins in warm seas; memories; children
who will remind us they never asked to be born.

Grasshoppers, June

The back gate of your long narrow garden
opened on nothing
but brambles, a steep impossibility

to where, far below, almost invisible,
the silent, disused
railway line ran, its inscrutable

elements heating in the sun, conducting
our childhood summers
north and south to Victorian platforms, their

dusty queues of nettles and saplings. The half-
inch grasshoppers
of June, they lay on the palms of our hands

for showing, look, folded like miniature
intricate pocket-knives
in their slender cases of fawn.

The small boys in the garden collecting them
are absorbed, a little
solemn. Indoors, the last of your tea

is stewing on a low blue flame. I am
almost as old as
you were then. Down all the long garden you

are calling us in, stopped creatures that jumped
at noon in our hands.
The railway line in two directions ran and ran.

The Weather at the End of the News

Our first flat in that delicate, drawn
city. Our first city! A basement
bed-sitter with a whiff of coal
though it was all electric. And the dried-up
biscuit of a tabby cat, a long time
dead, in the little cellar I broke into.

And when it rained, that dampwood
smoke of gnats in the drainy
sunken yard. I suppose the air
was full of life, though we didn't
think of it like that. April, May, I walked
an evening maze of colonies and mewses

to fish the small river, always
the colour of beer, in a skywards trickle
of Iron Blues and Dark Olives. I never
caught a thing but I liked it, I liked it; one
foot in shallow water, the other in the deep
wet grasses of Warriston cemetery.

We loved and slept on the rickety pull-
down bed I made at the second attempt.
It was all just sticks and rope and
we didn't take it when we left. One Sunday
morning the old landlord brought us
honey on the comb. When he asked about

our studies, our young marriage, I think
we knew he was introducing us, strangely,
to ourselves. And when you wrote,
after twenty years, I couldn't help it
I wept, embarrassed, in private. Then
in another room, brightly lit, I watched

the weather at the end of the news,
pulling myself together, secretly,
like something else I'd tried my hand at
hardly knowing where to begin; another thing
I'd jerry-built with loose hinges and strings,
and wouldn't want to take with me.

The Guests

You can't make them leave, though they wear you out
like children, demanding to be taken
to bright, wide-open fields, or shores of darkly wetted stones
where they never feel the cold, and love
the thrilling stink of ozone.

So you find the time and go, and sit behind them,
feeling the chill climb into your bones,
watching the slow, heavy machinery of ocean.
They are never bored, but after dark you ferry them back again,
a cargo of whispers.

And every time (half asleep at the wheel) you miss the unmarked
turn for home – the streets and rooms
you're already forgetting. You stop, always, in empty country,
the engine purring, and know they are content at last,
sleeping. And you wonder

where have you come to, so far from anything?
Why is this enough for them?

Dead Hawk, the Anglican Churchyard, Tangier

It is lighter at the tips
of my fingers than
the snap-out balsa planes
I made as a boy

and launched from
my bedroom window
on afternoons of Welsh rain
to a bare strip of garden.

Days of sun and wind
have whittled it clean
to stiff pinion
feathers and bone.

Cats stalk the desiccated
grasses between
the graves, but none of them
have dismantled it;

it has only been
troubled from within,
and all the hidden turmoil
that churned there is done.

The ebony crescent
of its beak is still
precise and fine. I can
see clean through

the empty house
of the skull,
like the quality
of a memory

the mind has refined,
to the gardener
with his combing rake,
who like the cats

has let it lie,
and to the dusty green
leaves above, and the
clean blue sky.

Not the Place but How the Place Was Found

Travelling lost is one way to get there
(not the place but how the place was found);
falling and lying all night is another.
The rooms that filled with snow, the quick black river
I fished and followed underground;
drowned bells in the loch at the heart of the moor.

Two beetles I poured from a graveside jar
were rowing to get there, round and round.
I know this road but not the places. Where your
house should stand is a foreign town.
Travelling lost is one way to get here.
Not the place but how the place was found.